THINK
STRAIGHT

ISBN: 9781973411529

THINK
STRAIGHT

Change Your Thoughts, Change Your Life

Written and Illustrated by

DARIUS FoRouX

TABLE OF CONTENTS

ABOUT THE AUTHOR (THAT'S ME)

I self-published this book, so it doesn't make sense to write this part in third person. To be honest, I *did* write an ego enhancing bio at first. I thought it looked more professional. But after I gave it more thought, I decided to do it differently and introduce myself the same way I do at an informal event.

Anyway, I'm an entrepreneur, blogger, and podcaster. For the past two and a half years, I've been sharing my thoughts about life, business, and productivity on my blog. Until now, more than 3 million people have read my articles. I also co-founded Vartex, a laundry technology company, with my dad, while I was finishing my master's degree in Marketing in 2010. For my podcast, The Darius Foroux Show, I've interviewed thought leaders like Ryan Holiday, Robert Sutton, Jimmy Soni, and more.

"If you can change your mind, you can change your life."

— William James

YOU BECOME WHAT YOU THINK

In 1869, a 27-year-old man, who had just graduated as a doctor of medicine from Harvard, was going through a "crisis of meaning." This was not the first time he dealt with adversity. Throughout his six years in medical school, his education was interrupted by different illnesses and bouts of depression. But this time, it was worse. He even contemplated suicide for months. The young man's name was William James, who later became the leading psychologist in America and one of the founders of the philosophical school of pragmatism. It took James three years to overcome depression. Something he did by himself.

To be clear, James wasn't just feeling down. John McDermott, editor of *The Writings of William James*, wrote about the severity of his mental state: "James spent a good part of life rationalizing his decision not to commit suicide."During this time, James also had panic attacks and hallucinations. This wasn't new to him. His father faced the same agonizing things, years before him. This feat made James believe that his condition was biological, and therefore something he couldn't overcome. But in 1870, James made a psychological breakthrough after reading an essay by Charles Renouvier, a French philosopher.

In his journal, he wrote: "I think that yesterday was a crisis in my life. I finished the first part of Renouvier's second Essais and see no reason why his definition of free will — 'the sustaining of a thought because I choose to when I might have other thoughts' — need be the definition of an illusion. At any rate, I will assume for the present — until next year — that it is no illusion. My first act of free will shall be to believe in free will."

This realization is at the core of pragmatism, the school of philosophy that James and Charles Sanders Peirce founded, years later. James realized that we have the ability to *choose* one thought over the other. In other words, we can control *what* we think.

However, James doesn't say we can control our consciousness. When we sit down and observe our thoughts for a few minutes, we will notice that a lot of things flow through our mind. The thoughts are just "there." Nothing we can change about that. But since we have free will, we can decide which thoughts we focus on. Hence, we can influence the direction of consciousness. This realization is critical to the way we live. It's the difference between "I can't help but feel this way" and "I feel this way because I *decided* to feel this way."

The emphasis is on *deciding*. And that's what this book is about: With practice, you can get better at controlling your thoughts so you can *decide* what you think.

And with better control over our thoughts, we can improve the quality of our lives and the outcome of our careers. That's my proposition in this book.

You have the ability to decide what you think. And since the result of your life depends on your thoughts, I think it's the most important thing in life. When we improve the way we think, nothing is impossible to achieve. That simple realization changes *everything*. Many great thinkers have written about the importance of thoughts. But William James' godfather, Ralph Waldo Emerson, who also inspired James a great deal, put it most simply: "You become what you think about all day long."

I believe that's true. But we must realize that actions follow thoughts. That means you can't change your actions without changing your thoughts. Let's start!

WHY DO WE NEED A BOOK ON PRACTICAL THINKING?

The human brain is the most important tool we have. It's more important than any technology, device, or instrument. Robert Greene, the author of Mastery, put it best: "If there is any instrument you must fall in love with and fetishize, it is the human brain—the most miraculous, awe-inspiring, information-processing tool devised in the known universe, with a complexity we can't even begin to fathom, and with dimensional powers that far outstrip any piece of technology in sophistication and usefulness."

However, there's one problem. We're born with this great tool, but we don't know how to use it properly. We're highly impractical beings. We think that we're good thinkers, but research paints a different picture. We think we make practical decisions that we base on logic. But that's not the case, as Dan Ariely, author of Predictable Irrationality, writes: "We usually think of ourselves as sitting in the driver's seat, with ultimate control over the decisions we made and the direction our life takes; but, alas, this perception has more to do with our desires—with how we *want* to view ourselves-than with reality." (emphasis mine)

It's safe to say we're not practical thinkers! The proof of that is the list of more than a hundred cognitive biases (or thinking errors) that scientists have found over the last century. We often make decisions based on gut feelings, emotions, and without having the right information. I've read several books about better thinking and decision making. I liked them. But I had one problem with all the books in this field: They weren't practical. They do a great job of describing *why* we think the way we think by sharing stories. But I couldn't find a practical book that explained *how* to change the way you think.

That's why I wrote this little book. It contains everything I've learned about thinking. My goal is to give you at least *one* idea that you can use to improve your thoughts, and consequently, your life, business, or career. That's why I share all my best ideas here. I wrote THINK STRAIGHT in a way that you can read it more than once. And I hope this book serves as an anchor to you—especially during trying times.

To keep this book practical, I combine theory, stories, and personal experiences to share advice you can apply (or not). The first idea I want to share is that these types of books only work if you're open-minded. If you think that's not you right now, I can save you an hour of your life. Just get rid of this book. Burn it, ask for a refund, give it away, whatever. No matter what you do, decide clearly: Use it or leave it.

USE WHAT WORKS

I'm not a neuroscientist, psychologist, philosopher, or any type of expert on the topic of "thinking." I'm a person who has lived his entire life under the impression that you can't control your thoughts. That way of thinking didn't serve me well. I was happy one day, sad the next. I got angry easily. And I couldn't find solutions to simple challenges I faced in my career, business, and relationships. But through experience, journaling, reading, and a lot of introspection, I've found a way to get better at thinking.

How do I know I'm better at thinking than before? I'm no longer a slave to my thoughts and I'm much happier because of it. I *use* my mind, and it's no longer the other way around. To me, that's the definition of better thinking. It has nothing to do with how smart you are or how many mathematical equations you can solve. It's about using your mind to get what you want.

I don't pretend to have all the answers to thinking better, though. However, I do have the answers to how *I've* used nothing but my thoughts to live a happier, healthier, wealthier, and more meaningful life.

I'm the living proof of the "change your thoughts, change your life" idea. Only three short years ago, I was stressed out of my mind, gave up my entrepreneurial desires, and hated my life. I felt stuck. But I don't want to be too dramatic about my situation. I think we've all been there. And if you haven't felt stuck in your life, it's only a matter of time before you will. It's a natural part of modern day life. I'm not trying to scare you, though. But you know how all these self-help books go, right? "I was down and out. I lost all my money. I was depressed. My life sucked. But then I discovered X. And then my life changed."

X is, of course, the idea they want to sell you. Since I'm honest with you, I'm no different. For example, in this book, I want to sell you on the idea of *useful* and *useless* thoughts. But there's a difference. I'm giving you my perspective—nothing more. It's up to you to decide what you're going to do with it.

John Dewey, a pragmatist, and one of the fathers of functional psychology, famously said: "The true is that which works." But that doesn't mean we should believe everything we hear or read. That makes us delusional.

If we want to *think straight* at all times, we must stay grounded, look at facts, listen to other people's perspectives, and only then draw practical conclusions.

CLEAR THINKING REQUIRES TRAINING

I view the mind as a muscle that requires regular training to keep strong. One way to train your mind is by learning new things. But I always thought that learning ends when your education ends. For some, that's when they leave high school, for others, it's when they get their bachelor's or master's degree. During our time in school, we learn new skills, ideas, and theories that change the way we think and operate in the world. But once we've established a way of thinking, we hardly change it. We prefer to entertain the same thoughts because they give us a sense of familiarity. We've learned that novelty is a scary thing—so we do everything to avoid it. We're creatures of habit who prefer *relaxing* our mind instead of *straining* it. "I need to relax and watch something on Netflix," is something I hear almost everyone, of all ages, say these days. I've said it myself as well.

That makes me wonder what we need rest from? From the repetitive tasks we do at work? From the familiar thought patterns we have? If you really think about it, we hardly strain our minds unless there's a specific reason—like a test or exam we *have* to take. Otherwise, we often think, "What's the point?"

Well, the point is to train your mind just like you train your body to keep fit. You don't go to the gym for four years and quit for the rest of your life. So why don't you exercise your mind the same way you do your body?

What's more, the mind is the single most important tool you have. And if you want to use that tool properly, you must train the mind. Stoic philosopher Epictetus put it best: "The life of wisdom is a life of reason. It is important to learn how to think clearly. Clear thinking is not a haphazard enterprise. It requires proper training."

The problem is that we don't know *how* we must get proper training, as Epictetus put it. For most of my life, my thoughts were out of control. I never thought about thinking. If you asked me to draw my thoughts, it would look something like this:

That mess you see up there is how the inside of my mind looked like. It was pure chaos. Just a mush of positive, negative, sad, happy and, above all, confusing thoughts. I always thought to myself, "Why can't my brain stop? Where's the pause button?" Looking back, I didn't know how to use my brain as the wonderful tool it is.

FROM CHAOS TO CLARITY

In 2014, I moved to London from Leeuwarden, The Netherlands, the city where I grew up. I went from a city with a hundred thousand people to a city where seven million people live. Things were harder than I expected. Especially when it came to finding a place to live. After doing research and talking to my new co-workers, I learned that it was almost impossible to find an apartment in a short period without getting ripped off. Instead, I decided to rent a room (which was a lot easier) for three months. And I decided to explore different areas in London that were within an hour commute by public transportation to my work. That was my plan. And everything went well. At first.

After two months, I found a small and affordable one-bedroom apartment in Earlsfield, in South-West London. I had planned everything. I canceled the lease of the room I rented, and signed the lease for the new apartment. My parents and brother even drove over from Holland to help out. And because I didn't have much stuff, we could just use their car to move my things from the old place to the new place, which were only 10 minutes apart. In my mind, this would be the deal: I would just pack up my stuff, get the key to the new place, hand the keys back to the old landlord, and move into the new place, watch Netflix and relax. Also, I expected to do everything on the *same* day.

Well, things didn't go as planned after all. My new landlady changed her mind last minute and decided not to rent out her apartment. She told me this a day before the day I planned the move. All of a sudden, I had no place to live and had an SUV full of my things. That night, in my parents' hotel room, I panicked. Big time.

"I don't know what to do! I have no place, my stuff is in a van, I brought you guys over from Holland, and now I'm sitting here like an idiot."

I continued blaming myself for the rest of the day and evening. You're probably thinking, "Really?" Yes, looking back on this, I can't help but think that I may have acted a little bit *too* dramatic. Well, let's just call it like it was: I was overdramatic. And not just a little. That's exactly why I picked out this example because it shows how stupid I was in my thinking. I spent so much time in my head that I had lost sight of the situation. I wasn't thinking clearly. And for what? Some first world problem? C'mon.

The next day, I woke up, and with the encouragements of my parents and brother, I decided to stop feeling sorry for myself and to start finding a solution instead. I said to myself, "THINK STRAIGHT."

I knew I had to replace the mess with clarity. I wanted to get straight to the point. I pictured this:

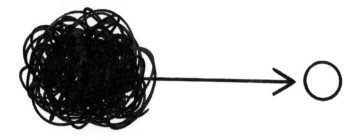

On the left: A mush of *useless* thoughts: Worry, stress, suffering, confusion, not knowing what to do.

On the right: ONE straight thought that has a (single) *useful* purpose. I wanted to start using my mind as a tool. In the case of my London story, I needed to look for a solution—fast.

It turned out that was easy, once I started thinking straight. I booked an Airbnb until I found a new place. In the end, we stayed in an Airbnb for a week. The landlady changed her mind *again* and decided to rent the apartment to me anyway.

So, all my stressing, worrying, and thinking were especially useless. How often does that happen? We're always so quick to judge and draw conclusions based on our assumptions. We're all human beings. We make mistakes. We change our minds. And we assume things that are not true all the time. That's normal. What's not normal is to let your mind go out of control.

And after many other useless thinking episodes, I decided to change. I didn't have *one* big epiphany or super dramatic moment that forced me to change. Life is not a Hollywood drama. People that I know only change after a *culmination* of problems. At some point, we stand up and say, "Enough." And you know what? A lot of people never change at all. But that shouldn't be our concern.

After years of chaos in my mind, I just had enough of mental suffering. I can't make it any prettier than that. You don't need an "all is lost" moment. Those type of moments almost never happen.

About two years ago, I started changing my thoughts. And I've learned to replace the chaos in my mind with clarity. Now, there's peace. In the rest of this book, I'll share with you exactly *how* I did it. But first, I want to share a brief history of thinking.

A (VERY) BRIEF HISTORY OF THINKING

Thoughts are important. But not all thoughts are equal. The quality of your thoughts matters the most. Roman Emperor and Stoic philosopher, Marcus Aurelius said it best: "The universe is change; our life is what our thoughts make it."

A quick look at our surroundings shows us that life is changing faster than ever. Jobs disappear, smartphones turn you into a zombie, education costs you thousands, the cost of living increases rapidly, salaries don't, you have less time for yourself, and so on. Life changes so fast that it seems like you wake up in a new world every day! What do your thoughts make of that? If you're anything like me, these developments cause a lot of thinking, aka worrying and uncertainty. How do I survive? How do I adapt my business to changing markets? How do I advance my career? How do I *not* lose my mind? Mastering your thoughts is challenging.

The desire to master our thoughts is as old as modern civilization. Ever since the fifth century BC, philosophers from all ages and regions agree on one thing: The human mind is an instrument that solves problems. And many philosophers argue that the quality of your thoughts determine the quality of your life. From Confucius to Socrates to Descartes to William James, they all talk about *their* method of thinking—a way to view the world.

Most of us know the Socratic method of questioning everything, even yourself. "I know one thing: That I know nothing," is what Socrates famously told the Oracle of Delphi when Socrates was declared the wisest man on earth. The fact that he thinks that he knows nothing makes him wise. That's a way of thinking.

French philosopher René Descartes, who lived in the 17th century, took it one step further. He questioned everything in life, even his own *existence*. Because how do you know you're not dreaming or living in The Matrix? That's why he famously said: "Cogito ergo sum." Popularly translated to, "I think, therefore I am." Descartes concluded that he must exist because he's able to think.

No matter how crazy your thoughts are, it's safe to say that you *do* exist. So why not make your existence a little more practical, lighthearted, fun, and useful?

Have you ever observed or written down your thoughts? I challenge you, try it for a day. Every two hours or so, sit down and write about what you're thinking at that very moment. Just don't get scared of yourself. Most of our thoughts make no sense at all. We're conflicted as a species. Descartes also reviewed his own thoughts and found many contradictions. His most important idea is that we should question the *source* of our beliefs, not the belief *itself*. Because most of our beliefs are based on our or other people's perception.

How many of your ideas are based on what others have told you? Or based on your first thoughts or assumptions? At the core of thinking lies our ability to separate the truth from falsehood. What is true, what is false?

One way to look at that question is to take a pragmatic perspective. William James describes the idea of pragmatism as follows: "The attitude of looking away from first things, principles, 'categories,' supposed necessities; and of looking towards last things, fruits, consequences, facts." **Thoughts should serve a useful purpose.** If they don't, they're useless. That's straight thinking.

Pragmatism is a method of thinking, not a solution. In fact, *all* thinking is a method. Your thoughts serve as an instrument. But it's a conflicting instrument that's very hard to use. Henry Ford said it best: "Thinking is the hardest work there is, which is probably the reason why so few engage in it." Thinking is not only hard—it's the single most important thing in life.

Remember: The quality of our thoughts determines the quality of our lives. And our decisions are a result of our thoughts.

LIFE IS NOT LINEAR

I always thought in a linear way: A leads to B. And if B is C, A also leads to C. I looked at appearances, first thoughts, and made a lot assumptions. But my thoughts didn't serve a useful purpose. In fact, they served no purpose at all. Instead of thinking, I followed convention. I let others do the thinking for me. Most of us are like that. For example, I thought I would never have to worry about having a job if I got my college degree.

I honestly believed that until I was about 26 years old. I figured out the hard way that nothing is guaranteed in life and that you have to work hard to earn money. And that making money has nothing to do with your degrees. If I had to pick another predictor of career success I would say it's skills. The better you are at something, the more value you can provide to others, and the more money people are willing to pay in exchange for your value.

Also, achieving a goal never happens linearly. Most of us believe there's a straight line from where you are to where you want to be. Let's say your goal is to start a business so you can have more freedom in your life. That was always my goal. I thought I would just work on it until I achieved it.

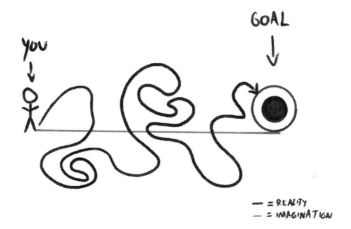

YOU

GOAL

— = REALITY
— = IMAGINATION

But that's not how it worked out. I had to take a lot of detours. I worked for many other people in between. I also started businesses that failed. Understanding that life is not linear helps us to change the way we think. Along the way, I got discouraged a lot and almost quit. Now, I realize that things often don't go according to plan. That helps me to think of backup plans or alternative options to get closer to my goals. Another personal goal of mine was to invest in real estate. When I lived in London and Amsterdam, that was difficult for me because I didn't have enough capital to get started. So instead of putting a lot of pressure on myself to make more money and sacrifice the quality of my life, I started looking elsewhere. After researching growing real estate markets, I ended up in my hometown.

Prices were low, I knew a lot of people, the population was increasing, and the city invested a lot in new businesses and education. Two months after I decided to look elsewhere, I bought my first deal there. The point is that there are multiple ways to achieve your goals. Also, if everyone is doing one thing, that often means you *shouldn't*.

CONNECT THE DOTS

Your brain is constantly working, even when you're not actively thinking. Apart from managing all the vital functions of your body, the brain also scans every piece of information that comes in. The brain compares it with other information that it has already stored. Your brain searches for similarities and differences between that information. That's how we think and use our brain to come up with new ideas. The brain consists of many small networks of neurons that connect to other networks, like this:

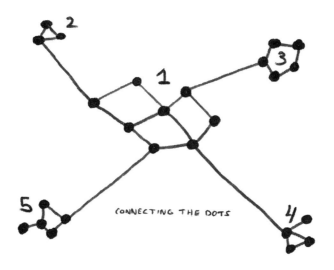

CONNECTING THE DOTS

Just a basic understanding of how my brain works helps me to understand how I can nurture it. I don't worry about finding a direct application for information I acquire. I feed my brain with knowledge that I'm curious about. And that diverse information might be stored in different networks, but as long as I connect the dots later, I'm okay with that. Like Steve Jobs said, "You can't connect the dots looking forward; you can only connect them looking backward. So you have to trust that the dots will somehow connect in your future."

If you want the dots to connect in the future, you have the make sure you *form* dots in your brain. The only way you form dots is by learning, doing, making mistakes, reflecting, or anything you can do to feed your brain with the input it needs to give you the output you want.

FILTER YOUR THOUGHTS

There's too much information in the world for our brain to process. So, we're forced to filter it. If we don't, we go nuts! And in that filtering-process, we develop shortcuts to ease the cognitive load of making decisions.

These shortcuts are called heuristics. A heuristic is a strategy we derive from previous experience with a similar problem. One heuristic that everyone knows is "trial and error," a strategy for finding answers to problems we face. It's also a way of thinking. But trial and error is not always the most *practical* strategy. If we would rely on trial and error to build a career, we would probably die before achieving that goal.

Life is too short for applying trial and error to everything. Another heuristic that's not practical is "social proof." We often make decisions based on what others do or say. And my favorite heuristic is "familiarity." It says that past behavior that led to good results is not a guarantee for future results. The familiarity heuristic also explains why we favor things and places we know over novelty. It's one of those things we see every day. We eat the same things, we walk the same route, we make the same mistakes, and we complete the same tasks at work. Over and over again. And then, we complain that our lives are stuck or boring.

No wonder, you're making decisions based on familiarity. But who says that familiarity is always a good thing? It's good for certainty. But to achieve a breakthrough, you need something different.

Making decisions based on heuristic techniques might ease the cognitive load, but they are far from practical. And often, heuristics lead to unsatisfying outcomes. If that's the case, take it as a sign that you must change something. Instead of relying on heuristics to filter information and make decisions, rely on the main idea of pragmatism: True is what *works*.

But don't take it too literally. "Taking drugs works for me," is what a contentious friend told me after I shared this idea with him. And he's right—you can't take this idea too literally. But what *can* you take literally in life? Take the platitude, "Good things come to those who wait," for example. I don't have to explain that it doesn't mean you should sit at home and wait forever until "good things" happen.

Look at the "true is what works" idea as a *filter* that you can apply to all the information that goes into your brain.

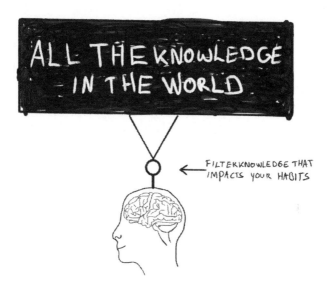

When faced with decisions, I ask myself: "Will the outcome of a decision change the way I live?" If you ask that yourself consistently, you'll find that you automatically filter out useless information and only make decisions that have an *actual* impact on the outcome of your life. You force yourself to use whatever works—what's useful. And what impacts your habits. For example, conventional thinking says that *bigger* cities also bring you *bigger* opportunities. I really thought that was true. That's even the main reason I moved to London. And yes, I did seize a big opportunity for me at the time.

But I also had bigger responsibilities and problems. Also, I don't like big cities. I hate crowded places, dirty air, and unreasonably high cost of living. Clearly, living in a big city didn't work for me. That way of thinking had a negative impact on the way I lived. That's why I eventually moved back to Leeuwarden. It's quiet, I know a lot of people here, I can work less, make more, and I can drive anywhere in the city within ten minutes. However, I also realize that for most people, my way of living doesn't work. They might find it boring or not exciting enough. So what? Do what works for *you*.

STOP "THINKING"

Thinking is difficult. I never knew how to stop. It's easy to stay inside your head for hours, especially when you're in bed at night. But I can confidently say that 99% of all my thoughts in the past have been useless. I didn't *do* anything with my thoughts most of the time. I didn't solve a problem. Nor did I try to understand difficult ideas or concepts from books. I spent a lot of time in my head doing this:

I called that thinking. But it was more like worrying, stressing, freaking out — call it whatever you want. I call it a preoccupied mind. And with what?

And the list goes on:

- "I wonder what my boss thinks?"

- "What happens if I screw up and lose my job?"

- "I think he doesn't care about me."

- "I just keep failing."

- "Does she love me?"

- "Why does my life suck?"

- "Why is my life awesome, and other people's lives are not?"

- "I don't care about my job. Is there something wrong with me?"

- "I can't finish anything. What's wrong with me?"

- "I want to quit."

I just have one question for you: What's the practical use of the above thoughts? Yes? I'm waiting. Still no answer? Exactly.

Those type of thoughts are not helping us. But we all have them. So how do you get rid of them? Well, I've learned that you can't get *rid* of them. Remember? We can't control our consciousness. We can only control what thoughts we follow through on.

You only have to be *aware* of your thoughts. Acknowledge them. But never blame yourself or say, "Why do I have these thoughts?" No one has the answer to that. It's better to be aware of your thoughts and decide what you will ignore, and what you will give importance to.

For example, the thought of quitting whatever I'm doing in my life has been on my mind as long as I remember. When I was in high school, I wanted to quit and just find a job. When I played basketball, I wanted to quit, and later did quit. I can go on and on until I reach the present. No matter how much I love what I do, the thought of quitting and just walking away shows up in my mind at least three or four times a month. In the past, those thoughts cost me many nights of sleep.

About two years ago I had enough. I wanted to quit thinking. So, I started becoming aware of my thoughts instead of always acting on every single thought I had. "You don't control me," I would say to myself like a weirdo. But it works. I'm much calmer and happier because of it. When I want to quit, I still listen to it because sometimes it *is* a sign. But more often, it's just fear. And I refuse to surrender to it. And neither should you.

INSIDE YOUR CONTROL VS OUTSIDE YOUR CONTROL

If you want to have useful thoughts, here's a rule of thumb: Only think about things you can control. That automatically eliminates about 99% of your thoughts because there's very little you control in life.

Only focus on what you control. Things like your:

- Desires
- Actions
- Words
- Intentions

What's a useless thought? Anything out of your control and *without* a useful purpose. Do you ever think about the past? That's the perfect example of a random thought that lacks a purpose, unless you're reflecting on a past decision or mistake you made. In the case of reflection, you're doing something useful. But other than that, every thought about the past serves no purpose. From that point of view, it's useless.

Ever fantasize about the future? That's also useless. I've discovered two main types of useful thoughts:

1. **Thinking about how you can solve problems.** A problem is just an unanswered question. Put your brain to use and think about how you can solve problems. There are a lot of those on this earth.

2. **Understanding knowledge.** That means this: Try to internalize knowledge and think about how you can use that knowledge to improve your life, career, work, relationships, etc.

That's it. You can ignore every other thought. If you're constantly thinking without a useful purpose, it's because you haven't' trained your mind yet. You have to get out of your head. If not, you'll go mental. Everyone will. No exception.

Ask yourself: "Is that worth it?"

Do you really want to waste your time, energy, and life on useless thinking? You and I both know the answer to that. **Commit to stop thinking about useless things. Start taking control of your mind.** All that worrying about the past and the future is not going to help you. It never did. And it never will.

DON'T TRUST YOUR MIND

Have you ever made a decision that seemed illogical looking back? We're very illogical beings. Every person creates their own social reality. The way you view the world is completely subjective because we all have cognitive biases.

The concept of cognitive biases was introduced in 1972 by two psychologists, Amos Tversky and Daniel Kahneman. A cognitive bias is a systematic thinking error that impacts judgments, and therefore, our decisions. My favorite cognitive bias is the "attentional bias." It's scientific evidence for the idea that your life is a result of your thoughts. The attentional bias states that our perceptions are affected by our thoughts. And naturally, our perceptions determine our actions and decisions, which make up our lives. If you have negative thoughts, you also have a negative perception of life. That's what it says. Our mind might be illogical, but it's also simple at the same time. Take one of the most well-known cognitive biases, the confirmation bias. It explains the behavior of confirming our preconceptions. If you believe in something, you will try hard to find information, clues, and signs to back that up. In other words, you do everything to prove you're *not* wrong. Instead of looking at facts, you look at *beliefs*. And that's what all cognitive biases do. As of this writing, there are 106 decision-making related cognitive biases known! I've read about most of them.

And I've read several books and studies about cognitive biases too. My conclusion is that your mind can't be trusted. Maybe my conclusion is also a cognitive bias. Who knows?

What it comes down to is this: Avoid making decisions based on beliefs, obvious logic, and even science.

Scientists are also human beings. That means they have *their* own cognitive biases. They are notorious for finding evidence for their preconceptions. The solution to making better decisions is not *more* knowledge. Instead, I've found that a pragmatic and neutral perspective leads to better-informed decisions. Unfortunately, there's no such thing as "the best decision." If that was the case, we lived in a perfect world full of people who made logical and practical decisions. I like to look at it this way: There are only *good-informed* and *bad-informed* decisions. It's very appealing to think we've got it all figured out because we've read a few books or studies. There's just one problem: You still can't trust your judgments, no matter how much knowledge you have. Being aware of that simple thought helps you make better-informed decisions. Every time I'm stuck in a thinking pattern, I try to break away by looking at the list of cognitive biases. It's free and easy. Just go to the Wikipedia for "list of cognitive biases." You'll find that most biases seem like common sense. And that's exactly the point. Cognitive biases explain our illogical behavior.

LOOK AT FACTS

I hate assumptions. And yet, I assume things all the time. When someone doesn't answer my email, I assume they don't care. When someone apologizes, I assume it's not genuine. When I have a headache, I assume I'm ill. I know I'm not practical because assumptions are not facts.

If you want to think straight, you discard all assumptions, and only look at facts. William James said it best in one of his lectures about pragmatism: "The pragmatist clings to facts and concreteness, observes truth at its work in particular cases, and generalizes."

To make things simple, let's look at two ways of making a decision. One based on facts, and the other based on assumptions.

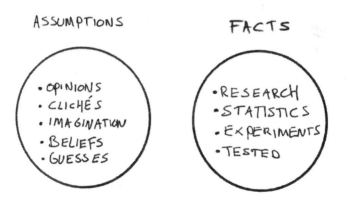

- Does your product solve a problem? Or do you assume it does?

- Are you able to raise money for your start-up? Or do you assume you will?

- Will you get a raise? Or do you assume your boss will give it to you?

- Is the sale a done deal? Or do you assume your client will sign?

- Do people like your art? Or do you assume they do?

I like to avoid assumptions as much as I can. I prefer to look at facts and then draw conclusions. What if you can't rely on facts? Well, sometimes you just can't find facts, or you have to make a quick decision. In those (very rare) cases I prefer gut feeling. Whatever you do, never waste your thoughts on *other* people's ill-informed opinions and guesses.

TRUE VS UNTRUE

In the previous chapter, we talked about looking at facts. But are facts also the truth? The answer is no. Confusing, right? It's just like life. For example, does God exist? I don't know. I've never seen any evidence. Does that mean God is not real? It doesn't matter what I think. If God has an impact on the way you live, it's true for you no matter what scientists say. Friedrich Nietzsche, the German philosopher who had a profound impact on western philosophy, famously said: "There are no facts, only interpretations."

Nietzsche was a man of true self-knowledge. Sigmund Freud even said that "he had a more penetrating knowledge of himself than any other man who ever lived or was ever likely to live." He was a very analytical thinker, especially when it came to his own thoughts. When Nietzsche said that there are no facts, he meant that we, as human beings, ultimately rely on our *interpretations* of reality. There's no way to confirm reality objectively. That doesn't mean nothing is real and that we're all living in a big dream. We just have to realize that facts are not the same thing as the truth. That simple thought saves you a lot of energy because it means no one can be right or wrong. Don't bother with convincing people with different opinions of the "truth." It's just not a practical thing to do. Save your energy for other, more useful things.

TAKE YOUR TIME TO THINK

I used to think that smart people are fast thinkers. "He thinks on his feet. He's really smart." I tried it for many years. Every time I faced a problem, discussion, or when someone asked me a question, I thought, "QUICK, QUICK, QUICK!" Naturally, my first answers sucked.

Derek Sivers, one of my favorite thinkers, says he's a slow thinker: "It's a common belief that your first reaction is the most honest, but I disagree. Your first reaction is usually outdated. Either it's an answer you came up with long ago and now use instead of thinking, or it's triggering a knee-jerk emotional response to something that happened long ago." Thinking things through takes time. Every time I gave a quick answer, I wasn't thinking at all, I was impulsive. Derek Sivers trained himself not to trust his first thoughts. That's also what he did when his email consumed too much of his time and attention. Being a public figure, Derek received a lot of emails from his readers. Most of them contained "quick 5-minute" questions. But as he says, if you get 100 of those questions, that adds up to 8 hours in a day. After answering 192,000 emails between 2008 and 2016, Derek knew he needed to do something about it.

So he planned to go off the grid like a modern-day Henry David Thoreau: "I was going to go hard-core, shut off all email and social media, and make myself unreachable to all but a few close friends and colleagues. It felt like the only solution."

That was his first thought. "But then I realized I could remain reachable as long as I don't answer questions," is what Derek writes on his blog (https://sivers.org/slow). I'm glad he didn't act on his first idea. His second idea is much better. I've emailed Derek myself in the past, and I think what he does makes a big impact on people's lives.

What I'm trying to say is that when someone asks you a question, it's okay to say, "I don't know." You can also say that to yourself. I've often been too hard on myself because I didn't have an instant answer to my personal problems. That doesn't make you dumb. It makes you human.

Why are we even afraid that people think we're stupid? It's the perfect example of slow thinking. Instead of following your instinct of, "I'll prove them!" you can take a step back and ask yourself, "Why do I even want to come across as smart?" If you really think about it, it doesn't matter what others think of you. I think it's always better to take your time to think. If others think that makes you stupid, they are the ones who are.

NO MORE QUICK DECISIONS

- "Shall we book a business trip to Thailand?"
- "Are you interested in a speaking gig at company X?"
- "Should we renovate the kitchen?"
- "Do you think we should fire John Doe?"
- "How about hiring another sales executive?"

Just a few questions others have asked me recently. And you know what? Just as I like to take time to think deeply about my challenges, I also take time to think "quick" decisions through. Every time I said yes to a speaking gig, interview, or giving a seminar, I didn't think about it for long. When things are in the future, we're more likely to say yes. "That trip is planned for September. It's now March. That's ages from now!" And without thinking about it, you commit to a five-day business trip or family vacation. But when September comes, you're either in a great professional flow, have other (more important) commitments, or are in the middle of something else. Now, all of a sudden, that quick yes from 'ages' ago is on your mind all the time. "Should I cancel the trip? Should I go? Should I go for two days only?"

Why do we make things so complicated while we can easily solve these things by just taking an extra day to THINK? That's all you need. Just think things through. Know yourself. For instance, I'm currently in a great writing flow. I don't feel the need to leave my city. I have a set routine every day, and it works very well for me. I feel happy, and I enjoy my life a lot. When I go away for even a weekend, my whole routine can be messed up. And then I need another two weeks to get back to my 'old' self.

However, I don't always have this mindset. Right now, I'm working on this book, opening a new office, and buying a new apartment. I'm focused on a few important things. But other times, I'm more flexible and actually do *like* to travel, visit friends, business partners, and live a looser lifestyle.

That's why I now take more time to make decisions. Instead of following my first thought, I say, "Please give me a day or two to think about it." That's all you need.

RELEASE YOUR MIND

Once I changed my perspective on life, I started straining my brain every single day. I started reading two hours a day and taking extensive notes of the things I learned. I also started writing articles to share the ideas I learned. In the beginning, I felt like a new world opened up to me. I couldn't get enough of learning more. I bought new books every week and devoured every piece of new knowledge I could get my hands on.

But after a few weeks, I had a mental breakdown. All of a sudden, my mind froze up. I felt blocked. I couldn't think, read, *or* write. My head hurt all day long. That went on for a few days, almost a week. I felt ill and I didn't understand why. I couldn't even *think* about why. And when I felt better, I just picked up where I left off. This time, I went on for longer, about two months before I hit another wall. But this time it was different again. No matter what I tried, I didn't feel like I was improving or learning new things. But I kept going and pushing through the difficulty. After this pattern occurred a few times, I finally understood what was going on. Training your mind happens in stages—and before you can move on to the next phase of your learning development, you have to get through a wall. I believe that both learning skills and developing yourself happen in stages.

At the beginning of a new stage, things are easy to learn because everything is new. But the closer you get to the end of a stage, things get more difficult. In my case, I got headaches. But I wasn't near the *end* yet because, after a short setback, I got back at it again.

At some point, you hit a big wall. That's the mental breakdown. It's also a point at which you want to give up whatever you're trying to achieve: Writing a book, starting a business, changing your career or leading a group of people. When you hit a wall, everything stops. The book all of a sudden seems useless, the business seems to fail, the career you want seems unreachable, and the people have stopped taking you seriously. All is lost.

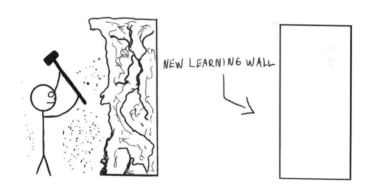

NEW LEARNING WALL

I've learned to train my brain to take this as a positive moment. When I reach a wall, I know I'm close to the next stage of my development. Instead of giving up, I'm happy. All I need to do, is to take a break, rejuvenate, and let my mind recover. I hang out with my friends. Play some table tennis with my brother at our office. Listen to my favorite artist like Jay-Z, Bob Dylan, Kendrick Lamar, or Bon Iver. Watch movies (a lot of them). I just take some time to relax and let my brain get stronger while I'm not thinking or working on anything. And then, I get back to where I left off. I use my energy to break through the wall. And it always works.

DRAW YOUR THOUGHTS

Before we invented language, we communicated and thought in images. But for many centuries, words have been our primary way to communicate. And that's why we also think in words. When I think, I talk to myself. And when I take notes, I also talk to myself.

"Create a chapter about drawing your thoughts," is what I wrote in my notebook when I came up with the idea for this chapter. I find that fascinating. One of the best-known thinkers of all time, Leonardo da Vinci, thought visually. How do I know this? I took a look at his notebooks, which you can easily find if you Google them. Here's an example:

Now, we don't have to become this great at drawing, but I think we can still learn something. Drawing frees your mind from the constant verbalization. I started drawing the images for my blog posts over a year ago. My drawing skills haven't improved, but my articles have. And one of the reasons is that I *take time* to think about how I can *visually* share my idea. I want readers to immediately "get" what I'm trying to share in the article by looking at my drawings.

That's why I think a lot about visualizing an idea. Sometimes I draw a graph, sometimes I emphasize a sentence or word, and I even make simple cartoons. After I make the drawing, I often edit my article to make my idea clearer. And some articles even start with a drawing.

This book also started with a drawing. It's the drawing I used in the From Chaos To Clarity chapter. Here it is again:

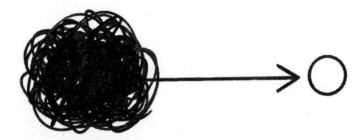

I made that drawing without a purpose. I was just visualizing some of my ideas. One of my ideas is that it used to be chaos in my mind, until I found a way to overcome it. As a result, I think clearly. That's the whole drawing. And now it's a book.

BE YOURSELF (NOT WHAT YOU SHOULD BE)

"Conquer yourself rather than the world."

— *René Descartes*

I'd like to ask you a few questions:

- What are you good at?
- What are you bad at?
- How do you learn new things?
- What are you passionate about?
- What do you dislike?

In other words: *Who* are you? What's your DNA? Sure, biologically we're all more or less the same. We all have organs, bones, blood, nerves. We also all die.

Why is self-knowledge important? I never had a clue. In all my years in school, no one ever talked about knowing yourself and why it matters. But it turns out that a lack of self-knowledge is the reason why I made the wrong decisions in my life.

- The jobs I had.
- The girls I dated.
- The things I chased.

- The decisions I made.
- The people I spent time with.

It didn't match with my strengths, values, skills, and desires.
My ex-girlfriend wanted to travel the world and live in
different countries. I hate that idea. I want to stay close to
my family and best friends. I don't feel like I'm missing out
on something if I don't live in other countries. Having a
home is what makes me happy. When you're in a
relationship with someone who has different values, it's a
zero-sum game. One person always loses something. We
broke up.

I've worked in boiler rooms, selling foolish products to
people who didn't need them. Why did I have a job that
made me feel bad about myself? I don't know. My best
guess is that I wanted the money. I thought that's what you
do. But I didn't know myself.

Today, I know myself better than I did ten years ago.
And in ten years from now, I'll know myself better than I do
today. Knowing yourself is step one. Step two is acting on
that knowledge.

Sometimes opportunities come my way and I feel like
saying yes too quickly. But I have to take a step back. And
ask myself: Is this really me? Very often, the answer is no.
I've found that most things in life are not for me. Most jobs,
opportunities, countries, people, parties, lifestyles, books—
they're all not for me. It's about finding the things that *are*
for me. Believe it or not, that's a very small list.

TAKE TIME TO REFLECT

We live busy lives. And sometimes there's no time for thinking. When thinking is not a priority, make it one. If you don't, you'll end up like me a few years ago. I didn't reflect on anything between 2012 and 2015. Result? All of a sudden, I felt overwhelmed and didn't know what to do with my life.

I had a true internal crisis on my hands. Since I had no idea what to do, I started reading more books. And I noticed that many smart and happy people kept journals. They also reflected more on their life. More specifically, they reflected on the things they learned, mistakes they made, and the goals they achieved.

When I started daily journaling, I began with writing my own autobiography. It's not meant for publication. It's meant for reflection and learning. If you don't know what to write about—write your life story. I'm sure you'll learn more about yourself with every paragraph you write.

I journal and make sure to read my notes once a week. That's all I mean when I talk about reflecting. I do it for three reasons:

1.   It helps me to uncover my mistakes so I can avoid them in the future.

2.   It helps me to value my progress when I read my past achievements.

3.   To get my thoughts in order so I can second guess myself. That helps me to make better decisions.

In short, I journal and reflect because it's useful.

MY MONEY RULES

One of my friends told me he hates his job. I asked him why he didn't take any action. "I need the money," he said. I automatically knew that he assumed that the only option for him is to quit. The reason is that we become too dependent on something when we give it too much importance.

There's a simple solution to devalue the value of money. I live by these five rules:

(PRACTICAL) **MONEY RULES**

* Don't buy shit you don't need.

* Save at least 10% of your income every month

* Stay out of Debt

* Invest your money in things that have a return

* Don't be stingy (It's just money)

That's what I've done for the past three years. And I haven't had a single thought about money. Actually, that's not true. I still *think* about money. Everybody does. But as soon as I think, "I have enough money in my savings account," I stop thinking about money. No matter what happens, if you have enough money to survive for six months, you'll figure it out.

There's only one condition: Invest in your skills. It's naïve to think we'll always be able to find a job or make money. It takes effort. But since when is that a surprise?

I just make sure I *invest* my money instead of *spending* it. Investing money is not only about investing in the stock market or in real estate. I have no problem paying three grand for a new laptop because it's a tool I use to do my job, and that makes me money. Also, I'm never cheap when it comes to buying important things. I'd rather buy a good jacket that lasts years than buy a cheap one that I have to replace next year.

Simply put, I don't buy things I don't need. I don't need a new iPhone every year. I also don't need five thousand dollar shoes. But that doesn't mean I own only one pair of shoes. I simply don't buy *everything* I like. Buying stuff in excess is not practical because I don't have enough space. Plus, I like to train myself to resist things to improve my self-discipline.

Remember: Money is a replaceable resource. When you're out of it, you can earn it back. You can't say the same for time. Don't spend too much time thinking about money.

DON'T TRY TO THINK YOUR WAY OUT OF EVERYTHING

This doesn't make sense at first sight, but when you think too hard, you often come up with bad ideas. That's because you can't actively think your way out of everything. We've all had good ideas while taking a shower. That's because we're not actively thinking.

It's good to let your attention wander and stop thinking. This is also a part of controlling your mind. You have the ability to decide when you want to let go of your thoughts. Similar to relaxing your muscles when you lay on the couch after a tough day, you can let loose of your thoughts.

You can do that in many different ways. Some like to take a yoga class. Others prefer to meditate every day. The medium doesn't matter. I've learned that there are many ways to relax. However, only one thing is critical: You don't *need* anything to relax but yourself.

You don't need yoga, exercise, meditation, music, scents, or whatever it is you think you need. Let go of everything. You can escape your outside world and go inside your mind to find peace. If you can't do that right now, train yourself. Become aware of your thoughts, observe them, and let them go. That's the whole process. You can do that anytime, anyplace.

You don't need a different scenery or class to do those things. Let go and relax. And do it as often as you think is necessary. You'll find that the moments you're *not* thinking are just as important as the times you are actively thinking.

BE UNCONVENTIONAL

I've grown to hate conventional thinking. Not because I want to be different but because conventional thinking gives you conventional results. I don't like that. And if *you* liked conventional results, you wouldn't be reading this book.

Let's examine decision making for a second. The most conventional method for decision making is to create a pros and cons list. Benjamin Franklin is the first who documented this method. He wrote about it to his friend, Joseph Priestley, in a letter to him in 1772. And today, we create these lists all the time. What are the pros and cons of...

- "Quitting my job?"
- "Breaking up with my boyfriend?"
- "Taking this job offer?"
- "Buying a new car?"
- "Starting a business?"

And then, we take a sheet of paper, draw a line in the middle of it, and start listing the pros on the left, and the cons on the right (or vice versa). Even though I like the simplicity of this method, I stopped using it after one of my friends recommended me to create one of these lists when my first relationship hit a rough patch.

I actually made a pros and cons list for breaking up with my then-girlfriend! When I think about it now, I'm ashamed. And it didn't even make any sense because there are always factors that, by themselves, outweigh all of the other factors. Nearly all pros and cons lists for relationships are the same.

- **Pros of staying in a relationship:** Having someone to share everything with, you can have sex, go on holidays, etc.
- **Cons of staying in a relationship:** Less free time for myself, getting in fights, going to in-laws, etc.

It's *always* the same. And it's not useful. The same is true for quitting a job you hate. The pro is that you're free from a bad job. The con is that there's a lot of uncertainty.

It's time to break free from this conventional thinking. Instead of binary thinking, start thinking more abundantly. **It's not *this* or *that* in life. You can have this *and* that.** I always thought I had to either quit my business or take a job. Also, many of my friends think you should quit your job to start a business. Who ever said these things?

When my business wasn't growing a few years ago, I just took a job at a large IT research firm. I did both things. I ran my business in the evenings and weekends (and sometimes during the day), and the rest of my time, I did my work for the firm. Also, you can start a business while you still have a job. That's what I mean when I talk about thinking outside of the box.

We always limit ourselves by narrow and conventional thinking. We always want to stay within a box. That's because we never take a step back to look at the larger picture. Take a look at the drawing below.

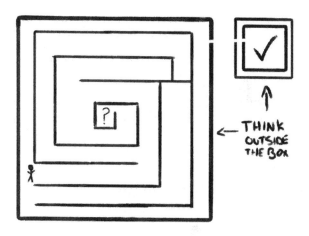

If you're standing inside the maze, you'll probably start walking towards the middle, right? That's what you *should* do when you're in a maze. However, this maze is different. The prize is not in the middle, it's outside the maze. But you can only see the goal if you take a helicopter view. It's impossible to see the goal from within the maze. And yet, that's how most of us live. We do things conventionally because that's "how it's done."

When you stop doing things the way they're done, you'll start doing things how *you* get it done.

DON'T ASK WHY

I'm a fool with sending emails. Especially when it comes to selecting the recipient. I always type the first letter of a name and hit enter. I trust the computer and never check whether the address I've selected is actually the person I want to mail. I'm lazy. Often, it doesn't matter and I get funny responses back from people.

But one time this simple mistake cost me $150K in business. I was working with two companies on a multi-year consulting deal. Both of my contacts had the same name, let's call them Wim. One Wim was an existing client, let's call him Wim A, and the other was a prospect, Wim B. Both guys wanted the same type of consulting for their companies. But I gave Wim A a better rate because he was a loyal customer. However, instead of sending the contract to Wim A, I sent the contract to Wim B.

This time, it wasn't an innocent mistake. Wim B previously had seen my proposal, which had a higher total price. But when he saw that Wim A got a lower rate, he was upset. "Why does he get a lower rate? Is that how you do business?" He decided not to do business with us. I learned three things.

1. Always double check.
2. Small things can become big things.
3. And don't play favors.

There's no use in asking why I made a mistake. Or why I was always lazy with email. I just was. And I was wrong. There's no way to justify my mistake. Never brush important details off and say, "It doesn't matter." Maybe it doesn't matter that you hit snooze every single day, or that you ignore the details of your book, report, or movie.

The point is that not striving for perfection becomes a habit. Don't worry about being a perfectionist—there's no such thing. More often than not, people are the opposite. Perfectionism is merely an excuse. In reality, we're scared of what people think of our work.

Either way, there's no point in asking "why" when you deal with obstacles, challenges, or mistakes. Instead, think about *what* you can do to overcome or prevent the things that are holding you back.

THINK ABOUT THE DETAILS EVEN MORE

I overlooked a small detail, and it cost me a lot. But the lesson I learned was more valuable than the business I could gain. Details are probably the most important thing in business, work, sports, art, and life in general. "The devil is in the detail." It's one of my favorite platitudes. But I never followed the advice in the past. The main reason was my impatience. I always tried to hurry everything: Sending emails, making calls, writing reports, assignments, essays, you name it. I thought that it mattered that I got the work done. But I was wrong. Because things often seem easy from the outside. Until you start doing them.

This book took me 15 months to write. I spent countless hours researching the topic. I also spent hours on writing, editing, cutting, writing more, and editing it again. And then, again. I also changed the title three times, and the subtitle even more than that.

My first title was The Art Of Practicality. I initially liked it a lot because it sounded familiar. But as I started writing a book about thinking, I also applied the methods to my own book. So I thought, "What does *the art of* even mean?" I didn't have a good answer. I took that as a sign that I needed to change the title. You know what's funny?

My second title was The Power Of Pragmatic Thinking. Like a genius, I came up with *another* generic title (which was even longer than the previous one)! Do you know how many books start with The Power Of? A quick book titles search on Goodreads with "the power of" gave me 83895 results. That's a lot of books with those words in the title or subtitle. One of the things I've learned about writing books is that you must stand out somehow. No one cares about a better book on thinking. Instead, it's likely that you picked up this book because you expected something *different*. But with the previous titles that I had drafted, I knew no one would *think* it'd be different.

Two weeks before I published THINK STRAIGHT, I started promoting it on my site and social media. And quickly, my readers became excited. Soon, emails like these came pouring in:

- "Can't wait for the book! Well done."
- "I am so excited to read your new book!!"
- "What a determined person you are! I look forward to Think Straight."

I love my readers. That's why I put in a lot of time to get the title right. At that time, no one had read the book. But based on the title, readers were already excited. And that was my goal. To everyone who emailed me before the launch: I hope I delivered ;)

Thinking about details is nothing more than doing your job. If you're a writer, your job is to write the best book you possibly can. If you're a designer, your job is to create the best design you can. You're not here to write one book and call it quits. Or to design one product and retire. If you want to grow—financially, spiritually, mentally—you must revisit the details all the time.

Never underestimate or overlook details if you want to do a job right. And if you don't, it's better not to do it at all.

TAKE THINKING OUT OF THE EQUATION

I don't want to become someone who only thinks and never acts. In fact, the only reason I think is that I want to do more with my life. I like to get more out of it because it gives me satisfaction. That's why I don't like to think on an average day. Sounds paradoxical, right? "You say you should think better, but now you're saying you're thinking less yourself."

That's exactly what I'm saying. Improve the quality of your *thoughts*, so you improve the quality of your *actions*. And always have an imbalance.

Action > Thinking

The best way to make sure you act more is to rely on habits. Take exercise. I've struggled with staying in shape for all my life. And I was overweight for years. I always played mind games with myself about exercise and diet.

- "Should I go for a run or go to the gym?"
- "I'll have this bag of chips and hit the gym tomorrow."
- "What days should I exercise? Mondays, Wednesdays, and Fridays? Or maybe Tuesdays and Thursdays?"

That's too much useless thinking. Instead, I've made a few basic rules:

- Exercise at least 30 minutes a day (*every day*)
- Don't burn yourself out (don't go all out)
- Eat healthy (no junk-food)
- Don't consume more calories than you burn
- Keep track of what you eat and how much you exercise

When you combine a few rules, you have a system. And a system helps you to take the thinking part out of the equation. The only thinking you need to do is when your system doesn't give you the results you want. If my system would make me feel bad or gain weight, I would rethink it. And even if it works, a system is never perfect. That's why I regularly think about what I can change or how I can improve my systems.

DON'T LIVE WITH REGRETS

Growing up, my grandmother was always around. She was a very kind person. Maybe too kind because she made many sacrifices in her life. For her parents, brothers and sisters, husband, and later on, her children. That's also a part of life. You can't live together and build a strong family without giving. But the biggest sacrifice she made was to live in The Netherlands for the last part of her life instead of her home country of Iran. As long as I remember, she always talked about the past. *Always*. And especially during the last few years of her life, she almost cried every day because of regret.

Fortunately, my mother, father, brother and I visited her often and cheered her up. But through the laughs, I could see the regret. It was always present. I've learned many lessons from my grandmother. Mostly about kindness and the importance of having strong family values. **But the most important lesson I've learned was that you don't regret what you *did* in life, you regret what you *didn't* do.** And when my grandmother passed away in January 2015, I decided to live by that lesson no matter what.

For example, I always thought I wanted to travel the world and live in different cities. I know, it's not an original goal. I speak to a lot of people who love that idea of freedom and exploration. Why is that? I think a lot of it comes from pop culture. A lot of people idolize people like Jack Kerouac and Ernest Hemingway, who were famous for their travels. And young folks now are inspired by social media personalities who also travel the world and share it on their Instagram feed. The medium might have changed, but the desire to travel to others and share your experiences with others has not. However, that lifestyle is not for everyone.

But I didn't know that before I actually started traveling. How could I? Some things in life you must experience to know what they're like in reality. No one can truly feel how it is to be an entrepreneur unless they start doing it. You can read all the business books you want, and watch as many videos about entrepreneurship as you want, but they will not *make* you an entrepreneur. Ever. You will only end up living someone else's life.

I'd rather eat rice and beans so I can do the things that I love instead of having a job that makes me miserable, but pays well. At the end of the day, this is your life and the only way you can live with yourself is to follow your strongest desires. Just make sure you think straight so you eventually *act* on those thoughts.

NEVER LOOK BACK

I hardly look back on life. I never daydream of the past. I don't look at old photos all day long. I don't even think about taking pictures because I'm too involved in the present. Sometimes, I feel like most people are stuck in the past. They live their life in the past tense. Instead of enjoying a moment, they grab their phone and take a picture of it. Instead of living life through a lens, I prefer to be present at all times. Now, I must be honest that I fail to be 100% present.

However, I intend to live *now*. And I know I'm successful because I never have the urge to relive the past. I'm too busy enjoying now. That doesn't mean I never stop to take a family picture. I just don't go around snapping millions of pictures that I will never look at again. Think about it, when do you have the time to take a look at all your memories? How many pictures and videos do you have? How many old documents, old diplomas, memorabilia, and other physical things do you have stored that remind you of the past?

If you're having a hard time letting go of the past, let me make it easier for you. You'll never going to…

- Use your first iPhone that you've kept in your desk drawer for years
- Edit that video from the weekend trip you took with friends

- Look at your old school papers, essays, and grades
- Wear those old clothes you have in storage
- Do anything with the object that reminds you of your first date

When we hold on to a lot of things in the past, they form an obstacle to living in the present. The only useful purpose I can think of for looking back is to learn. You can draw many lessons from looking at your past. That's why I like to journal. I regularly go back to my journal entries to understand my thought process at the time. Especially when something doesn't work out the way I want, I go back and try to understand why. For example, in 2017, after two years of regular blogging, and building up a newsletter with more than 22.000 members, I decided to start a paid membership site. Before I started the membership site, I contemplated it excessively. "If I get 1000 readers to support me with $5 a month, I can make a living off writing, training, and helping others. The paid members will get exclusive content from me. That's a good value proposition." That was my thinking process. I came up with the number 1000 because of Kevin Kelly's seminal article, 1000 True Fans. I also studied how other bloggers started their membership sites.

Everything looked good on paper. And I had sold hundreds of online courses before that, so I knew people valued my work.

But things didn't turn out as I expected. After a month, 78 people signed up. After six weeks, I pulled the plug on the membership site. Many of my friends, colleagues, and even paid members told me I stopped too quickly. Maybe so. However, I'm not the type to quit when things are hard. I've thought about quitting education many times during my 6,5 years when I was getting two degrees. I also thought about quitting my family business many times because it's very hard to make a living. But that's never going to change. No, instead, I quit my membership site because I thought straight: "At this rate, it takes me more than 12 months to get 1000 paid members. Plus, within the first month, half a dozen people canceled. So if I take cancellations into account, it will take me even longer. Also, during the past six weeks, I've felt an obligation to provide exclusive content to my paid members. I want them to get something out of the membership. That pressure costs me a lot of time that I could spend on growing our family business or my coaching practice. All in all—a membership site is not the right strategy for me." Instead of making a simple calculation of 1000/78, I thought further than that. How can you get people to stay? How much work does it take you? And what are alternative ways of achieving my goals? There are many other ways I can help others.

There are also many other ways for me to make a living. That's why I decided to pull the plug on my membership site after only six weeks. If things don't work out, it's not the end of the world. Make a decision. Stand by it. Move on. And only look back to learn.

When I look back on my experiment with starting a membership site, I could've easily prevented myself from wasting a lot of time. It took me about three months to create the membership area, create content, write copy, etc. Before I started, I knew that it would take time to run a membership site. Remember the chapter about details? If you want to do a job, do it right or not at all. In this case, I should have done nothing at all. Why? Because I spend too much time on running my family business, writing articles, books, creating courses, and consulting. From looking back, I've learned that I can only take on one big project per every aspect of my life.

So yes, look back, but don't stare for too long. Life happens now.

SPEND YOUR TIME WELL

Time is limited. Sooner or later we all figure that out. And once we do, we start being more conscious of the way we spend our time. Thinking is a double-edged sword. It can help you. But it can also destroy you. The outcome depends on how you use your thoughts. Your mind is an instrument—nothing more, nothing less. In this book, I shared how I've learned to use my brain more effectively. Sometimes you have to think differently, and there are times you must stop thinking altogether. It's up to you to decide when you should deploy which method. But no matter what you do, don't spend too much time in thought because that's a waste of life. At the end of the day, thinking by itself is useless without action. But like we talked about earlier, action follows thought.

Effective thoughts? Effective actions.

To clarify what I mean, I've made a list of what I think are effective thoughts:

- Making your life better
- Growing your career and business
- Visualizing your future
- Thinking of new ideas
- Solving problems

- Coming up with fun things to do with your partner, family, or friends

It's really not that complicated. However, sticking with this way of thinking is very hard and takes work. Don't expect to become a practical thinker after reading this book only once. Like any skill, better thinking requires daily practice. I do that by looking at everything that happens in my life as an exercise for thinking better.

Because if I don't, I start wasting my time on useless things like complaining, feeling sorry for myself, and not enjoying my life.

We're collectively thinking so much we're missing out on life. And it has nothing to do with fancy things other people do. We all know that the beauty of life lies in the small things. Did you notice the sunshine this morning when you woke up? Or the raindrops? Did you notice the smell of your coffee? Did you feel the texture of your cereals?

If your answer is no, you definitely need to get out of your head. **Stop thinking and start feeling.**

INNER CALM

There's only one end goal to all of this: Inner calm. No matter what you experience in life, and no matter what happens to you, your mind should stay calm under all circumstances.

That's the ultimate prize in life. Mastery of the mind means that we control our mind. Remember: You can only achieve that through *daily* practice. Some people call it meditation and others might call it mindfulness. No matter what you call "finding inner calm," please don't overcomplicate it. You don't need a ten-thousand-dollar course to learn how to find some peace inside your head.

Just sit down, be one with your thoughts, observe them, and then, *ignore* them. That's all there is to meditation.

I "meditate" all the time—when I walk, exercise, write, wait, sit, lay, whatever. I can always find the time and energy to go within myself to find peace. I don't need anything to do it. That's important to realize. I've said it before. But it's so important that I'll say it again: You *don't need* a yoga mat, music, or teacher to help you control your thoughts. You can go within yourself to find calm *anytime* you want. You also don't need a holiday, new shoes, or a drink.

How do I know this? I control my mind. I decide what it does. **So can you.**

THINK BEYOND YOURSELF

Many of the ideas I shared in this book come from the philosophy of pragmatism. If you Google 'pragmatism', you'll probably read that the philosophical movement was founded by Charles Sanders Peirce, a former professor at Johns Hopkins University. But if you look closer into the story behind the philosophy, you'll find that it was William James who actually credited Peirce as the founder in 1898.

Even though Charles Sanders Peirce was a well-respected academic during the 1880s, he had fallen from grace by the end of the 19th century. James and Peirce got to know each other during the 1860s when they were both students at the Lawrence Scientific School at Harvard. Peirce, once considered as a prodigy of mathematics and logic, went on to become a professor at Johns Hopkins University. But he lost his position in 1884 due to a scandal involving his re-marriage. It's truly a sad story. Peirce's first wife left him in 1875 and shortly after that, he became involved with another woman, while still being legally married. However, his divorce became final eight years later. During those eight years, he lived with a woman he was not married to. Apparently, Simon Newcomb, who was Peirce's colleague, told on him. Consequently, he was let go in what became a public scandal.

Sadly, Peirce never found academic employment again and lived in poverty for years after he was fired. Peirce even lived and slept on the streets of New York City for years.

No one helped him, except for his old friend William James. After James overcame his depression in 1870, he started building a body of work that, more than a century later, remains relevant. James became a Harvard professor and an academic celebrity due to the publication of his book, Principles of Psychology. A book that took him twelve years to write and was published in 1890. In contrast to his friend, James' career was on the rise for years.

And out of nowhere, in 1898, William James credited "the principle of pragmatism" to the forgotten Charles Sanders Peirce, in a lecture called "Philosophical Conceptions and Practical Results." Pragmatism means that one must look at the practical value of ideas. James believed scientists wasted their time on abstract ideas and theories that had no impact on people's lives. Would you change the way you lived if a scientist proved how the earth was created? Louis Menand, author of *Pragmatism: A Reader*, says of the principle of pragmatism that, "We can never hope for *absolute* proof of anything. All our decisions are bets on what the universe is today, and what it will do tomorrow." Regardless of what people think of pragmatism, one thing is sure: William James did a favor to Peirce by crediting the philosophy to him. And that is exactly what makes James great.

He didn't strive to take credit for something that *he* created. Because without James' actions and promotion of pragmatism, the philosophy wouldn't exist and Peirce would be forgotten.

By that act, James did something meaningful—he helped a friend. Peirce gained some respect and even wrote several papers in his last years. And from all the wisdom of James, that's the most important thing I've learned.

William James himself once said: "The greatest use of a life is to spend it on something that will outlast it." Practically speaking, there's no purpose to doing something that outlasts you. You won't be there to see it anyway. But that's not the point. If we *live* our lives every day with that idea in mind—that we should strive for doing/creating useful things that matter to *others*—we end up spending our time on things that actually make a difference. When you do that, life automatically has meaning—to everyone.

THANK YOU: A GIFT

Thank you for going on this journey with me. My goal was to take you *inside* my thinking process. I hope that this book serves as an anchor to you and that you read it more than once. Especially during trying times.

I appreciate that you took the time to finish THINK STRAIGHT. Deciding to read one book over the other might seem small to a reader who has millions of options, but to me, the author, it means everything.

So, thank you.

To show you my gratitude, I want to offer you something in return: A bonus eBook with a behind the scenes look at my personal journal entries. In the bonus eBook for THINK STRAIGHT, I take you one step deeper into the creative journey.

If you enjoyed this book, and want to know how it was made, go to DariusForoux.com/THINK-STRAIGHT-BONUS to subscribe to my newsletter and download the bonus for free.

I hope we can continue this conversation about how to think better. Therefore, I invite you to share your story with me, personally or on my site's community page, where other readers share *theirs*.

I like to build real relationships with my readers. That's why I always ask people to stay in touch.

My desire is to see other people do well in life. So, please, go out there, and make good shit happen. And then, let me know about it!

Take care,
Darius

FURTHER READING

Pragmatists like William James, Charles Sanders Peirce, and John Dewey didn't view themselves as philosophers. In fact, they believed that most of philosophy was useless. Even though we might call them philosophers today, they had other professions. Throughout history, pragmatic thinkers had occupations like judges, educators, politicians, and poets.

Instead of talking endlessly about which philosophy is best, they *used* the ideas of pragmatism to live a better life. And to live a good life, you don't need endless study of philosophy. Instead, we must act! That's why I've kept the further reading of this books short.

If you want to read more about pragmatic thinking, I recommend reading William James' work. He is by far my favorite pragmatic thinker. The biography of James by Ralph Barton is also a great view inside his practical mind, and contains his journal entries.

If you just want to read one book on pragmatism in general, I recommend Louis Menand's book, which contains several important texts from the most important pragmatist philosophers. In his book, Menand also shares an insightful introduction that reveals more about the core ideas of pragmatism.

Enjoy!

- Pragmatism and Other Writings by William James
- The Thought And Character Of William by Ralph Barton Perry
- Pragmatism: A Reader by Louis Menand

70816405R00054

Made in the USA
Middletown, DE
17 April 2018